A SHORT

CONFESSION

OF FAITH

A SHORT CONFESSION OF FAITH

Benjamin Keach

𝜋𝜌 PARRĒSIA

A Short Confession of Faith
© 2021 by Parrēsia Ltd.

ISBN 978 1 8382829 2 9

This book was edited and designed by Daniel Funke,
with assistance from John-William Noble.

Typeset in Adobe Garamond Pro
and Adobe Garamond Premier Pro

Printed in Glasgow by Bell & Bain Ltd.
Cover art: © Cute Designs / Adobe Stock

parresiabooks.org

Editor's Note

The text of Keach's *Short Confession* is taken from the original edition published in 1697. We have made a number of small changes related to spelling and punctuation. We have also sought to correct a number of the Scripture proofs, where these were clearly wrong; these instances are marked with an asterisk (*). In other cases, we chose to omit Scripture proofs that were clearly wrong and where we could not reasonably be certain what Keach sought to reference.

We have followed Keach's numbering of the Articles. In all but two instances, the numbers are tied to the headings for the articles. The two exceptions are Articles 2 and 18, where an ornament (∽) is placed above, and the number is placed at the beginning of the paragraph.

While this short book has immense value in understanding Particular Baptists at the end of the seventeenth century, we publish it with the hope that it would benefit Christians and churches today.

—THE EDITOR

A SHORT CONFESSION OF FAITH

The Articles of Faith of the Church of Christ, or Congregation, meeting at Horsley-down, containing the substance of all the fundamental articles in the Larger Confession, put forth by the elders of the baptized churches, owning personal election and final perseverance.

But this I confess unto thee, that after the way which they call heresy, so worship I the God of my fathers, believing all things which are written in the law and in the prophets.—Acts 24:14.

London, 1697

THE EPISTLE DEDICATORY

To the Congregation with whom I am a member (and the unworthy overseer) who are in God the Father, and in our Lord Jesus Christ; grace, mercy and peace be multiplied.

Most Dear and Beloved in Christ:

I HOPE I can say (with the holy apostle) that you are by me dearly beloved, my joy, and my crown; yea you are my honour, and in you I would rejoice, being the ornament of my poor ministry, by which the most of you have (through the blessing of God) been converted to Jesus Christ: and if you stand fast in the faith in one spirit, striving together for the faith of the gospel, and do adorn your profession, living in love, and endeavouring to keep the unity of the Spirit in the bond of peace, you will cause my latter days to be most sweet and comfortable to me, after all those troubles, sorrows, and reproaches I have met with, both from within and from without. Evident it is God hath most eminently appeared to strengthen your hands: though the archers have sorely grieved you, and shot at you, yet your bow abideth in strength; and that the arms of your hands may still abide strong by the arm of the mighty God of Jacob, shall be my continual prayers.

My brethren, I here present you with that which you have so long waited for, and desired me to endeavour to do, viz. to state an account of the most concerning articles of your faith, which you have heard read, and have approved of, and which I thought good no longer to delay the doing of.

1. Not knowing how soon I may put off this tabernacle, and therefore would leave behind me an account of that holy doctrine and order, in which through grace you are established (for at your desire also I have drawn up the whole rules of your holy discipline, which you may have added unto this, and bound up together).

2. And the rather I have done this, because the general and more large confession of the faith of our churches, is now out of print; but that is not all, for that being 12 d. price, some cannot well purchase it.

3. And also that all men may see what our faith is, and that we differ not from our brethren who bear other names in any fundamental point or article of faith; and that they may discern the difference between you and some that bear the same name with you.

4. Though you agree in the general with all other churches of the same Faith, in all those Articles there inserted, yet therein your whole faith is not comprehended, viz. that of imposition of hands upon baptized believers as such, and singing of God's praise, etc., because some of our churches dissent from us therein: yet my desire is you would nevertheless show all tenderness, charity and moderation to such as differ from you in those cases, and not refuse communion with them; and indeed your late sweet temper appears to be such, that I need not press you to this. All that I shall say more, is to entreat you to labour after holiness, and to awake out of sleep, that you may adorn your sacred profession, and prepare to meet the Lord; that as you have a good doctrine, you may also have a holy and good conversation; and then we need not fear who can harm us, whilst we are followers of that which is good, O let us bear one with another. And if in any thing we differ, let us avoid all animosities. Brethren, great things are near, watch and pray, look out and be ready. But at present I shall conclude with the words of the Apostle, 'Finally, brethren,

farewell. Be perfect, be of good comfort, be of one mind, live in peace; and the God of love and peace shall be with you.'

So prays your unworthy brother, pastor, overseer, and servant, who earnestly desires your prayers also.

B. Keach

From my house in Freemans-lane
by Horsley-down, Southwark.
August 16, 1697.

That the following Articles contain what the foresaid Church believes concerning those truths asserted therein, we whose names are hereunto subscribed, do testify in the name and by the appointment of the whole congregation, the 10th day of the 6th Month, commonly called August, 1697,

Benjamin Keach, Pastor,
Benjamin Stinton, Teacher,
John Roberts, Deacon,
Edward Foley, Deacon,
Joshua Farrow, Deacon,
Tho. Stinton, Deacon,
John Valley, Deacon,
Isaac Ballard, Deacon,
John Hoar, Sen.,
Edward Newbury,
Tho. Turner,
John Seamor,
Ephraim Wilcocks,
James Wilmott,
Daniel Dines,
Richard Thoubals,
John Weston,
John Clark,
Tho. Ayers,
John York,
George Starkey, Sen.,
Benj. Harris,
George Starkey, Jun.,
John Beavis,
Tho. Hill,
Joseph Berry,
William Farmworth,
Joseph Jennings,
John Fowle, Sen.,
Tho. Fowle,
John Fowle, Jun.,
Henry Skeer,
John Greensmith,
Jeremiah Lions,
William Putman,
Nath. Holden,
William Cattrel,
Tho. Harvey,
Tho. Richford,
Joseph Worley,
Peter Carter,
William Forister,
Sam. Cox,
John Sparke,
James King,
William Deale,
Simon Agars,
John Hoar, Jun.,
Tho. Gunning,
William Mais.

THE ARTICLES OF FAITH OF THE CHURCH OF CHRIST MEETING AT HORSLEY-DOWN

1. Of God, and of the Holy Trinity

WE DO BELIEVE, declare and testify, that there is but one only living and true God, who is a Spirit infinite, eternal, immense and unchangeable in his being, wisdom, power, holiness, justice, goodness, truth and faithfulness.

John 4:24 God is a Spirit: and they that worship him must worship him in spirit and in truth. **Job 11:7** Canst thou by searching find out God? canst thou find out the Almighty unto perfection? **8** It is as high as heaven; what canst thou do? deeper than hell; what canst thou know? **9** The measure thereof is longer than the earth, and broader than the sea. **Psa. 90:2** Before the mountains were brought forth, or ever thou hadst formed the earth and the world, even from everlasting to everlasting, thou art God. **Jas. 1:17** Every good gift and every perfect gift is from above, and cometh down from the Father of lights, with whom is no variableness, neither shadow of turning. *****Exod. 3:14** And God said unto Moses, I AM THAT I AM: and he said, Thus shalt thou say unto the children of Israel, I AM hath sent me unto you. **Rev. 4:8** And the four beasts had each of them six wings about him; and they were full of eyes within: and they rest not day and night, saying, Holy, holy, holy, Lord God Almighty, which was, and is, and is to come. **Deut. 6:4** Hear, O Israel: The Lord our God is one Lord. **Exod. 34:6** And the Lord passed by before him, and proclaimed, The Lord, The Lord God, merciful and gracious, longsuffering, and abundant in goodness and truth, 7 Keeping mercy for thousands, forgiving iniquity and transgression and sin, and that will by no means clear the guilty; visiting the iniquity of the fathers upon the children, and upon the children's children, unto the third and to the fourth generation.

∼

2. That there are three persons in the Godhead, the Father, the Son, and Holy Spirit; and that these three are one God, the same in essence, equal in power and glory.

Matt. 28:19 Go ye therefore, and teach all nations, baptizing them in the name of the Father, and of the Son, and of the Holy Ghost. **1 John 5:5** Who is he that overcometh the world, but he that believeth that Jesus is the Son of God?

3. Of the Decrees of God

THAT THE DECREES of God are his eternal purpose according to the counsel of his will, whereby for his own glory he hath foreordained whatsoever comes to pass, even those evils that his wisdom and justice permit for the manifestation of the glory of those his attributes: And that God executes his decrees in the works of creation and providence.

Eph. 1:4 According as he hath chosen us in him before the foundation of the world, that we should be holy and without blame before him in love. **11** In whom also we have obtained an inheritance, being predestinated according to the purpose of him who worketh all things after the counsel of his own will. **Rom. 9:22** What if God, willing to shew his wrath, and to make his power known, endured with much longsuffering the vessels of wrath fitted to destruction: **23** And that he might make known the riches of his glory on the vessels of mercy, which he had afore prepared unto glory.

4. Of Creation

THAT THE WORKS of creation are God's creating all things of nothing by his word of power, in six days, and all very good. That God created man male and female, after his own image, in knowledge, righteousness, and holiness, with power and dominion over the creatures.

Gen. 1. Heb. 11:3 Through faith we understand that the worlds were framed by the word of God, so that things which are seen were not made of things which do appear.

Gen. 1:25 And God made the beast of the earth after his kind, and cattle after their kind, and every thing that creepeth upon the earth after his kind: and God saw that it was good. **27** So God created man in his own image, in the image of God created he him; male and female created he them. **28** And God blessed them, and God said unto them, Be fruitful, and multiply, and replenish the earth, and subdue it: and have dominion over the fish of the sea, and over the fowl of the air, and over every living thing that moveth upon the earth.

Col. 3:10 And have put on the new man, which is renewed in knowledge after the image of him that created him. **Eph. 4:24** And that ye put on the new man, which after God is created in righteousness and true holiness.

5. Of God's Providence

WE BELIEVE THAT God's works of providence are his most holy, wise, and powerful preserving, and governing all his creatures, and their actions.

6. Of the Holy Scriptures

WE BELIEVE THE holy scriptures of the Old and New Testament are the word of God, and are the only rule of faith, and practice; all things being contained therein that are necessary for us to know concerning God, and our duty unto him, and also unto all men. That all persons ought to read, hear, and understand the holy scriptures. That the light of nature, and works of providence, though they declare plainly there is a God, yet not so effectually as the holy scriptures; nor can we know without them how, and in what space of time God created all things. Neither came we any other ways but by the holy scriptures to the knowledge of Christ the blessed Mediator; which indeed none can savingly know but by the word and Spirit of God.

> **2 Tim. 3:16** All scripture is given by inspiration of God, and is profitable for doctrine, for reproof, for correction, for instruction in righteousness. **Eph. 2:20** And are built upon

the foundation of the apostles and prophets, Jesus Christ himself being the chief corner stone. **John 5:39** Search the scriptures; for in them ye think ye have eternal life: and they are they which testify of me. **Deut. 17:18** And it shall be, when he sitteth upon the throne of his kingdom, that he shall write him a copy of this law in a book out of that which is before the priests the Levites. **Rev. 1:3** Blessed is he that readeth, and they that hear the words of this prophecy, and keep those things which are written therein: for the time is at hand. **Acts 8:30** And Philip ran thither to him, and heard him read the prophet Esaias, and said, Understandest thou what thou readest?

Gen. 1. Gen. 3:15 And I will put enmity between thee and the woman, and between thy seed and her seed; it shall bruise thy head, and thou shalt bruise his heel. **16** Unto the woman he said, I will greatly multiply thy sorrow and thy conception; in sorrow thou shalt bring forth children; and thy desire shall be to thy husband, and he shall rule over thee.

John 20:30 And many other signs truly did Jesus in the presence of his disciples, which are not written in this book: **31** But these are written, that ye might believe that Jesus is the Christ, the Son of God; and that believing ye might have life through his name. **John 21:24** This is the disciple which testifieth of these things, and wrote these things: and we know that his testimony is true.

7. Of Original Sin

WE DO BELIEVE, that God having created man, he entered into a covenant of life with him, upon the condition of perfect obedience; making the first Adam a common head to all his seed: and that our first parents being left to the freedom of their own will, fell from the estate wherein they were created, by eating of the forbidden fruit: and that Adam being set up as a public person, we all sinned in him, and fell with him into a state of sin, of wrath and misery; the sinfulness of which state consists in the guilt of Adam's first sin, the want of original righteousness, and the corruption of our whole nature: from whence all actual sins proceed, as water out of a filthy and an unclean fountain. So that not only by imputation all men became sinners in the first Adam, but also as the same corrupt nature is conveyed to all his posterity, who descend from him in ordinary generation.

> **Gen. 3. Gen. 6. Eccl. 7:29** Lo, this only have I found, that God hath made man upright; but they have sought out many inventions. **Rom. 3:23** For all have sinned, and come short of the glory of God. **1 John 3:4** Whosoever committeth sin transgresseth also the law: for sin is the transgression of the law. **Titus 1:13** This witness is true. Wherefore rebuke them sharply, that they may be sound in the faith. **Rom. 5:17** For if by one man's offence death reigned by one; much more they which receive abundance of grace and of the gift of righteousness shall reign in life by one, Jesus Christ. **Gen. 6:5** And God saw that the wickedness of man was great in the earth, and that every imagination of the thoughts of his heart was only evil continually. **Jer. 17:9** The heart is deceitful above all things, and desperately wicked: who can know it? **Rom. 3:10-18. Jas. 1:14** But every man is tempted, when he is drawn away of his own lust, and enticed. **1 Cor. 15:21** For since by man came death, by man came also the resurrection of the dead. **22** For as in Adam all die, even so in Christ shall

all be made alive. **Rom.** 5:6 For when we were yet without strength, in due time Christ died for the ungodly. **Rom.** 8:7 Because the carnal mind is enmity against God: for it is not subject to the law of God, neither indeed can be. **Col.** 1:21 And you, that were sometime alienated and enemies in your mind by wicked works, yet now hath he reconciled. **Matt.** 15:19 For out of the heart proceed evil thoughts, murders, adulteries, fornications, thefts, false witness, blasphemies. **Rom.** 7:7 What shall we say then? Is the law sin? God forbid. Nay, I had not known sin, but by the law: for I had not known lust, except the law had said, Thou shalt not covet. **14** For we know that the law is spiritual: but I am carnal, sold under sin. **17** Now then it is no more I that do it, but sin that dwelleth in me. **18** For I know that in me (that is, in my flesh,) dwelleth no good thing: for to will is present with me; but how to perform that which is good I find not. **23** But I see another law in my members, warring against the law of my mind, and bringing me into captivity to the law of sin which is in my members. **24** O wretched man that I am! who shall deliver me from the body of this death? **Lam.** 3:39 Wherefore doth a living man complain, a man for the punishment of his sins? **Rom.** 6:23 For the wages of sin is death; but the gift of God is eternal life through Jesus Christ our Lord. **Gal.** 3:10 For as many as are of the works of the law are under the curse: for it is written, Cursed is every one that continueth not in all things which are written in the book of the law to do them.

Job 11:12 For vain man would be wise, though man be born like a wild ass's colt. **Job** 15:14 What is man, that he should be clean? and he which is born of a woman, that he should be righteous? **Job** 25:4 How then can man be justified with God? or how can he be clean that is born of a woman?

By this sin all mankind lost the image of God, and communion with him, being liable to all the miseries of this life, and to death itself; and also are dead in sins and trespasses, and obnoxious to the wrath of God, and the eternal pains of hell forever. Hence we say that all are conceived and born in sin, and are the children of wrath, even the elect as well as others, being wholly defiled in all the faculties and parts of soul and body, and utterly indisposed and disabled to do anything that is spiritually good, and wholly inclined with a strong propensity to all things that are evil.

Col. 3:10 And have put on the new man, which is renewed in knowledge after the image of him that created him. **Titus 1:13** This witness is true. Wherefore rebuke them sharply, that they may be sound in the faith. **Ps. 51:5** Behold, I was shapen in iniquity; and in sin did my mother conceive me.

Eph. 2:2 Wherein in time past ye walked according to the course of this world, according to the prince of the power of the air, the spirit that now worketh in the children of disobedience: **3** Among whom also we all had our conversation in times past in the lusts of our flesh, fulfilling the desires of the flesh and of the mind; and were by nature the children of wrath, even as others.

Gen. 6:3 And the LORD said, My spirit shall not always strive with man, for that he also is flesh: yet his days shall be an hundred and twenty years. **Rom. 7:5** For when we were in the flesh, the motions of sins, which were by the law, did work in our members to bring forth fruit unto death. **14** For we know that the law is spiritual: but I am carnal, sold under sin. **15** For that which I do I allow not: for what I would, that do I not; but what I hate, that do I. **16** If then I do that which I would not, I consent unto the law that it is good. **17** Now then it is no more

I that do it, but sin that dwelleth in me. **23** But I see another law in my members, warring against the law of my mind, and bringing me into captivity to the law of sin which is in my members. **24** O wretched man that I am! who shall deliver me from the body of this death?

8. Of Man's Free-will

WE BELIEVE MAN in his state of innocency had freedom of will to do good; but by the fall he hath utterly lost all that power and ability, being woefully depraved in all the faculties of his soul; there being in the will and mind of all naturally much enmity against God, and a total aversion to him, and to every thing that is spiritually good; loving darkness, and rebelling against the light.

> **Eph. 2:2** Wherein in time past ye walked according to the course of this world, according to the prince of the power of the air, the spirit that now worketh in the children of disobedience: **3** Among whom also we all had our conversation in times past in the lusts of our flesh, fulfilling the desires of the flesh and of the mind; and were by nature the children of wrath, even as others.
> **Rom. 8:7** Because the carnal mind is enmity against God: for it is not subject to the law of God, neither indeed can be.
> **Job 24:13** They are of those that rebel against the light; they know not the ways thereof, nor abide in the paths thereof.

But when a man is renewed by divine grace, though there is no force put upon the will, yet it is made willing, and acts freely, in the day of God's power: though the work is not perfect in any faculty in the regenerate, nor will be in this life.

Eph. 4:28 Let him that stole steal no more: but rather let him labour, working with his hands the thing which is good, that he may have to give to him that needeth.

Col. 1:21 And you, that were sometime alienated and enemies in your mind by wicked works, yet now hath he reconciled. **Ps. 110:3** Thy people shall be willing in the day of thy power, in the beauties of holiness from the womb of the morning: thou hast the dew of thy youth. **Rom. 7:11** For sin, taking occasion by the commandment, deceived me, and by it slew me. **17** Now then it is no more I that do it, but sin that dwelleth in me. **18** For I know that in me (that is, in my flesh,) dwelleth no good thing: for to will is present with me; but how to perform that which is good I find not. **23** But I see another law in my members, warring against the law of my mind, and bringing me into captivity to the law of sin which is in my members. **24** O wretched man that I am! who shall deliver me from the body of this death?

9. Of Christ the Mediator

WE BELIEVE THAT God having, out of his own mere good pleasure, and infinite love, elected some persons of the lost seed of the first Adam unto everlasting life, from all eternity, did enter into a covenant of grace with the second person of the Trinity (who was set up as the common head of all the elect), to deliver them out of the state of sin and misery, and to bring them into a state of salvation and eternal happiness.

Eph. 1:4 According as he hath chosen us in him before the foundation of the world, that we should be holy and without blame before him in love. **Rom. 3:20** Therefore by the deeds of the law there shall no flesh be justified in his sight: for by the law is the knowledge of sin. 21 But now the righteousness of God without the law is manifested, being witnessed by the law and the prophets; 22 Even the righteousness of God which is by faith of Jesus Christ unto all and upon all them that believe: for there is no difference. **Gal. 3:21** Is the law then against the promises of God? God forbid: for if there had been a law given which could have given life, verily righteousness should have been by the law. 22 But the scripture hath concluded all under sin, that the promise by faith of Jesus Christ might be given to them that believe. **1 Tim. 2:5** For there is one God, and one mediator between God and men, the man Christ Jesus; 6 Who gave himself a ransom for all, to be testified in due time. **John 1:14** And the Word was made flesh, and dwelt among us, (and we beheld his glory, the glory as of the only begotten of the Father,) full of grace and truth. **Gal. 4:4** But when the fulness of the time was come, God sent forth his Son, made of a woman, made under the law.

Rom. 9:5 Whose are the fathers, and of whom as concerning the flesh Christ came, who is over all, God blessed for ever. Amen. **Luke 1:35** And the angel answered and said unto her, The Holy Ghost shall come upon thee, and the power of the Highest shall overshadow thee: therefore also that holy thing which shall be born of thee shall be called the Son of God. **Col. 2:9** For in him dwelleth all the fulness of the Godhead bodily. **Heb. 7:24** But this man, because he continueth ever, hath an unchangeable priesthood. 25 Wherefore he is able also to save them to the uttermost that come unto God by him, seeing he ever liveth to make intercession for them.

That the second person in the Godhead (being the eternal Son of God, co-essential, and co-equal with the Father), according to that holy covenant and compact that was between them both, became man, or assumed our nature, and so was, and continueth to be God and man in two distinct natures, in one person forever. And that he the Son of God by his becoming man, did take unto him a true body, and reasonable soul, being conceived by the Holy Spirit in the womb of the virgin, and was born of her, yet without sin.

> **Phil. 2:6** Who, being in the form of God, thought it not robbery to be equal with God. **Zech. 6:13** Even he shall build the temple of the Lord; and he shall bear the glory, and shall sit and rule upon his throne; and he shall be a priest upon his throne: and the counsel of peace shall be between them both.
>
> **John 1:14** And the Word was made flesh, and dwelt among us, (and we beheld his glory, the glory as of the only begotten of the Father,) full of grace and truth. **1 Tim. 2:5** For there is one God, and one mediator between God and men, the man Christ Jesus. **Heb. 2:14** Forasmuch then as the children are partakers of flesh and blood, he also himself likewise took part of the same; that through death he might destroy him that had the power of death, that is, the devil.
>
> **Luke 1:27** To a virgin espoused to a man whose name was Joseph, of the house of David; and the virgin's name was Mary. **31** And, behold, thou shalt conceive in thy womb, and bring forth a son, and shalt call his name Jesus. **34** Then said Mary unto the angel, How shall this be, seeing I know not a man? **35** And the angel answered and said unto her, The Holy Ghost shall come upon thee, and the power of the Highest shall overshadow thee: therefore also that holy thing which shall be born of thee shall be called the Son of God. **Gal. 4:4** But when the fulness of the time was come, God sent forth his Son, made of a woman, made under the law. **Heb. 4:15** For we have not

an high priest which cannot be touched with the feeling of our infirmities; but was in all points tempted like as we are, yet without sin.

10. Of the Offices of Christ

WE BELIEVE THAT the Lord Jesus Christ, who is our Redeemer, and the one blessed Mediator between God and man, executeth a threefold office, both the office of a priest, the office of a king, and the office of a prophet.

1 Tim. 2:5 For there is one God, and one mediator between God and men, the man Christ Jesus.

First, that he executeth the office of a priest, (1.) In his once offering up himself a sacrifice, to satisfy divine justice, and to reconcile God to us, and us to God. (2.) And in making continual intercession for us, that the merits of his blood may be made effectual unto us.

Heb. 2:17 Wherefore in all things it behoved him to be made like unto his brethren, that he might be a merciful and faithful high priest in things pertaining to God, to make reconciliation for the sins of the people. **Heb. 7:24** But this man, because he continueth ever, hath an unchangeable priesthood. **Acts 15:14** Simeon hath declared how God at the first did visit the Gentiles, to take out of them a people for his name. **15** And to this agree the words of the prophets; as it is written, **16** After this I will return, and will build again the tabernacle of David, which is fallen down; and I will build again the ruins thereof, and I will set it up.

1 **John 2:2** And he is the propitiation for our sins: and not for ours only, but also for the sins of the whole world. **Heb. 7:25** Wherefore he is able also to save them to the uttermost that come unto God by him, seeing he ever liveth to make intercession for them. **Heb. 10:21** And having an high priest over the house of God. **Heb. 9:24** For Christ is not entered into the holy places made with hands, which are the figures of the true; but into heaven itself, now to appear in the presence of God for us.

Secondly, that he executeth the office of a king in subduing us unto himself, and in giving us laws and holy precepts, by which we ought to walk; and also in his restraining and conquering all his, and our enemies.

Isa. 33:22 For the LORD is our judge, the LORD is our lawgiver, the LORD is our king; he will save us. **Isa. 32:1** Behold, a king shall reign in righteousness, and princes shall rule in judgment. 2 And a man shall be as an hiding place from the wind, and a covert from the tempest; as rivers of water in a dry place, as the shadow of a great rock in a weary land. **1 Cor. 15:25** For he must reign, till he hath put all enemies under his feet. *Ps. 110.

Thirdly, that he executeth the office of a prophet, in revealing to us by his word and Spirit, the whole will of God concerning all things that appertain to faith and practice.

Acts 3:22 For Moses truly said unto the fathers, A prophet shall the Lord your God raise up unto you of your brethren, like unto me; him shall ye hear in all things whatsoever he shall say unto you. **John 1:18** No man hath seen God at any time;

the only begotten Son, which is in the bosom of the Father, he hath declared him. **1 Pet. 1:10** Of which salvation the prophets have enquired and searched diligently, who prophesied of the grace that should come unto you: **11** Searching what, or what manner of time the Spirit of Christ which was in them did signify, when it testified beforehand the sufferings of Christ, and the glory that should follow. **12** Unto whom it was revealed, that not unto themselves, but unto us they did minister the things, which are now reported unto you by them that have preached the gospel unto you with the Holy Ghost sent down from heaven; which things the angels desire to look into. **John 15:15** Henceforth I call you not servants; for the servant knoweth not what his lord doeth: but I have called you friends; for all things that I have heard of my Father I have made known unto you. **John 20:31** But these are written, that ye might believe that Jesus is the Christ, the Son of God; and that believing ye might have life through his name.

11. Of Christ's Humiliation and Exaltation

WE BELIEVE THAT Christ's humiliation consisted in that great condescension of his in assuming our nature, and being born in a low condition, made under the law, undergoing the many miseries of this life, the wrath of God, the curse of the law, and the ignominious death of the cross, continuing under death for a time.

Gal. 4:4 But when the fulness of the time was come, God sent forth his Son, made of a woman, made under the law. ***Heb. 12:2** Looking unto Jesus the author and finisher of our faith; who for the joy that was set before him endured the cross, despising the shame, and is set down at the right hand of the throne of God. **3** For consider him that endured such contradiction of sinners against himself, lest ye be wearied and faint in your minds. **Isa. 53:2** For he shall grow up before him as a tender plant, and as a root out of a dry ground: he hath no form nor comeliness; and when we shall see him, there is no beauty that we should desire him. **3** He is despised and rejected of men; a man of sorrows, and acquainted with grief: and we hid as it were our faces from him; he was despised, and we esteemed him not. **Luke 22:44** And being in an agony he prayed more earnestly: and his sweat was as it were great drops of blood falling down to the ground. **Matt. 27:46** And about the ninth hour Jesus cried with a loud voice, saying, Eli, Eli, lama sabachthani? that is to say, My God, my God, why hast thou forsaken me? **Phil. 2:8** And being found in fashion as a man, he humbled himself, and became obedient unto death, even the death of the cross. **1 Cor. 15:4** And that he was buried, and that he rose again the third day according to the scriptures. **Acts 2:24** Whom God hath raised up, having loosed the pains of death: because it was not possible that he should be holden of it. **25** For David speaketh concerning him, I foresaw the Lord always before my face, for he is on my right hand, that I should not be moved: **26** Therefore did my heart rejoice, and my tongue was glad; moreover also my flesh shall rest in hope: **27** Because thou wilt not leave my soul in hell, neither wilt thou suffer thine Holy One to see corruption. **31** He seeing this before spake of the resurrection of Christ, that his soul was not left in hell, neither his flesh did see corruption.

And that his exaltation consisteth in his rising again from the dead the third day, and in his ascending up into heaven, in sitting at the right hand of God; angels, powers, and principalities being made subject unto him; and in his being made Judge of the quick and dead.

1 Cor. 15:4 And that he was buried, and that he rose again the third day according to the scriptures. **Mark 16:19** So then after the Lord had spoken unto them, he was received up into heaven, and sat on the right hand of God. **Eph. 1:20** Which he wrought in Christ, when he raised him from the dead, and set him at his own right hand in the heavenly places. **Acts 1:11** Which also said, Ye men of Galilee, why stand ye gazing up into heaven? this same Jesus, which is taken up from you into heaven, shall so come in like manner as ye have seen him go into heaven. **Acts 17:31** Because he hath appointed a day, in the which he will judge the world in righteousness by that man whom he hath ordained; whereof he hath given assurance unto all men, in that he hath raised him from the dead. **1 Pet. 3:22** Who is gone into heaven, and is on the right hand of God; angels and authorities and powers being made subject unto him.

12. Of Effectual Calling

WE DO BELIEVE that we are made partakers of the redemption purchased by Christ, by the effectual application of his merits, etc., unto us by the Holy Spirit, thereby uniting us to Christ in effectual calling: And that effectual calling is the work of God's free grace, who by his Spirit works faith in us, who are altogether passive therein; and convincing us of sin and misery, enlightening our minds in the knowledge of Christ, and renewing our wills, and changing our whole hearts, he doth persuade and enable us to embrace Jesus Christ freely, as he is offered in the gospel.

John 1:11 He came unto his own, and his own received him not. **Titus 3:5** Not by works of righteousness which we have done, but according to his mercy he saved us, by the washing of regeneration, and renewing of the Holy Ghost; **6** Which he shed on us abundantly through Jesus Christ our Saviour. **Eph. 1:13** In whom ye also trusted, after that ye heard the word of truth, the gospel of your salvation: in whom also after that ye believed, ye were sealed with that holy Spirit of promise, **14** Which is the earnest of our inheritance until the redemption of the purchased possession, unto the praise of his glory. **1 Cor. 1:9** God is faithful, by whom ye were called unto the fellowship of his Son Jesus Christ our Lord. **Eph. 2:8** For by grace are ye saved through faith; and that not of yourselves: it is the gift of God.

Eph. 3:17 That Christ may dwell in your hearts by faith; that ye, being rooted and grounded in love.

1 Cor. 1:9 God is faithful, by whom ye were called unto the fellowship of his Son Jesus Christ our Lord. **2 Tim. 1:9** Who hath saved us, and called us with an holy calling, not according to our works, but according to his own purpose and grace, which was given us in Christ Jesus before the world began.

2 Thess. 2:13 But we are bound to give thanks alway to God for you, brethren beloved of the Lord, because God hath from the beginning chosen you to salvation through sanctification of the Spirit and belief of the truth: **14** Whereunto he called you by our gospel, to the obtaining of the glory of our Lord Jesus Christ. **Acts 2:37** Now when they heard this, they were pricked in their heart, and said unto Peter and to the rest of the apostles, Men and brethren, what shall we do?

***Acts 26:18** To open their eyes, and to turn them from darkness to light, and from the power of Satan unto God, that they may receive forgiveness of sins, and inheritance among them which are sanctified by faith that is in me. **Ezek. 36:27** And I will put my spirit within you, and cause you to walk in my statutes, and ye shall keep my judgments, and do them. **John 6:44** No man can come to me, except the Father which hath sent me draw him: and I will raise him up at the last day. **45** It is written in the prophets, And they shall be all taught of God. Every man therefore that hath heard, and hath learned of the Father, cometh unto me.

13. Of Justification

WE DO BELIEVE justification is a free act of God's grace, through that redemption which is in Christ (who, as our head, was acquitted, justified, and discharged, and we in him, when he rose from the dead), and when applied to us, we in our own persons are actually justified, in being made and pronounced righteous, through the righteousness of Christ imputed to us; and all our sins, past, present, and to come, for ever pardoned; which is received by faith alone. And that our sanctification, nor faith itself, is any part of our justification before God; it not being either the habit, or act of believing, or any act of evangelical obedience imputed to us, but Christ, and his active and passive obedience only, apprehended by faith: and that faith in no sense tends to make Christ's merits more satisfactory unto God; but that he was as fully reconciled and satisfied for his elect in Christ by his death before faith as after; otherwise it would render God only reconcilable (not reconciled), and make faith part of the payment or satisfaction unto God, and so lessen the merits of Christ, as if they were defective or insufficient. Yet we say, it is by faith that we receive the atonement, or by which means (as an instrument) we come to apprehend and receive him, and to have personal interest in him, and to have our free justification evidenced to our own consciences.

Rom. 3:23 For all have sinned, and come short of the glory of God; **24** Being justified freely by his grace through the redemption that is in Christ Jesus: **25** Whom God hath set forth to be a propitiation through faith in his blood, to declare his righteousness for the remission of sins that are past, through the forbearance of God; **26** To declare, I say, at this time his righteousness: that he might be just, and the justifier of him which believeth in Jesus.

Eph. 1:6 To the praise of the glory of his grace, wherein he hath made us accepted in the beloved. **7** In whom we have redemption through his blood, the forgiveness of sins, according to the riches of his grace. **Titus 3:7** That being justified by his grace, we should be made heirs according to the hope of eternal life.

Rom. 5:15 But not as the offence, so also is the free gift. For if through the offence of one many be dead, much more the grace of God, and the gift by grace, which is by one man, Jesus Christ, hath abounded unto many. **16** And not as it was by one that sinned, so is the gift: for the judgment was by one to condemnation, but the free gift is of many offences unto justification. **17** For if by one man's offence death reigned by one; much more they which receive abundance of grace and of the gift of righteousness shall reign in life by one, Jesus Christ. **18** Therefore as by the offence of one judgment came upon all men to condemnation; even so by the righteousness of one the free gift came upon all men unto justification of life.

1 Cor. 1:30 But of him are ye in Christ Jesus, who of God is made unto us wisdom, and righteousness, and sanctification, and redemption. **2 Cor. 5:21** For he hath made him to be sin for us, who knew no sin; that we might be made the righteousness of God in him.

Acts 13:39 And by him all that believe are justified from all things, from which ye could not be justified by the law of Moses. **2 Cor. 5:21** For he hath made him to be sin for us, who knew no sin; that we might be made the righteousness of God in him.

Phil. 3:7 But what things were gain to me, those I counted loss for Christ. **8** Yea doubtless, and I count all things but loss for the excellency of the knowledge of Christ Jesus my Lord: for whom I have suffered the loss of all things, and do count them but dung, that I may win Christ, **9** And be found in him, not having mine own righteousness, which is of the law, but that which is through the faith of Christ, the righteousness which is of God by faith.

Rom. 10:5 For Moses describeth the righteousness which is of the law, That the man which doeth those things shall live by them.

14. Of Adoption

WE BELIEVE ADOPTION is an act of God's free grace, whereby such who were the children of wrath by nature, are received into the number, and have right to all the privileges of the sons of God; and that such who are adopted, are also by the Spirit regenerated, and hence said to be born of God.

1 John 3:1 Behold, what manner of love the Father hath bestowed upon us, that we should be called the sons of God: therefore the world knoweth us not, because it knew him not.

***John 1:12** But as many as received him, to them gave he power to become the sons of God, even to them that believe on his name. **Rom. 8:14** For as many as are led by the Spirit of God, they are the sons of God. **Gal. 2:16** Knowing that a man is not justified by the works of the law, but by the faith of Jesus Christ, even we have believed in Jesus Christ, that we might be justified by the faith of Christ, and not by the works of the law: for by the works of the law shall no flesh be justified. **1 John 3:1** Behold, what manner of love the Father hath bestowed upon us, that we should be called the sons of God: therefore the world knoweth us not, because it knew him not. 2 Beloved, now are we the sons of God, and it doth not yet appear what we shall be: but we know that, when he shall appear, we shall be like him; for we shall see him as he is. **1 John 4:7** Beloved, let us love one another: for love is of God; and every one that loveth is born of God, and knoweth God. **1 John 5:1** Whosoever believeth that Jesus is the Christ is born of God: and every one that loveth him that begat loveth him also that is begotten of him.

15. Of Sanctification

THAT SANCTIFICATION IS the work of God's free grace also, whereby we are renewed in the whole man after the image of God, and are enabled more and more to die unto sin, and live unto righteousness. And that the benefits we receive, and which flow from or accompany justification, are adoption, sanctification, peace of conscience, manifestations of God's love, joy in the Holy Ghost, an increase of grace, an assurance of eternal life, and final perseverance unto the end.

> **2 Thess. 2:13** But we are bound to give thanks alway to God for you, brethren beloved of the Lord, because God hath from the beginning chosen you to salvation through sanctification of the Spirit and belief of the truth. **Eph. 4:13** Till we all come in the unity of the faith, and of the knowledge of the Son of God, unto a perfect man, unto the measure of the stature of the fulness of Christ. **Rom. 6:5** For if we have been planted together in the likeness of his death, we shall be also in the likeness of his resurrection: **6** Knowing this, that our old man is crucified with him, that the body of sin might be destroyed, that henceforth we should not serve sin. **7** For he that is dead is freed from sin. **Rom. 8:29** For whom he did foreknow, he also did predestinate to be conformed to the image of his Son, that he might be the firstborn among many brethren. **30** Moreover whom he did predestinate, them he also called: and whom he called, them he also justified: and whom he justified, them he also glorified. **Rom. 5:1** Therefore being justified by faith, we have peace with God through our Lord Jesus Christ: **2** By whom also we have access by faith into this grace wherein we stand, and rejoice in hope of the glory of God. **5** And hope maketh not ashamed; because the love of God is shed abroad in our hearts by the Holy Ghost which is given unto us. **Rom. 14:17** For the kingdom of God is not meat and drink; but righteousness, and peace, and joy in the Holy Ghost. **Prov. 4:18** But the path of the just is as the shining light, that shineth more and more unto the perfect day. *****1 John 5:13** These things have I written unto you that believe on the name of the Son of God; that ye may know that ye have eternal life, and that ye may believe

on the name of the Son of God. **1 Pet. 1:5** Who are kept by the power of God through faith unto salvation ready to be revealed in the last time.

16. Of the Souls of Men at Death

WE BELIEVE, THAT at death the souls of believers are made perfect in holiness, and do immediately pass into glory; and their bodies dying in union with Christ, or dying in the Lord, do rest in their graves till the resurrection, when they shall be raised up in glory. And that their souls being reunited to their bodies, they shall be openly acknowledged, and acquitted, and made completely blessed, both in soul and body, and shall have the full enjoyment of God to all eternity. And that the souls of the wicked at their death are cast into hell, or are in torment: and that their bodies lie in the grave under wrath, and shall by virtue of the power of Christ be raised from the dead; and their souls being re-united to their bodies, shall be judged and condemned, and cast into a furnace of fire, or into unspeakable torment, with the devil and his angels, for ever and ever.

> **1 Cor. 15:43** It is sown in dishonour; it is raised in glory: it is sown in weakness; it is raised in power. **Matt. 25:23** His lord said unto him, Well done, good and faithful servant; thou hast been faithful over a few things, I will make thee ruler over many things: enter thou into the joy of thy lord. **Matt. 10:32** Whosoever therefore shall confess me before men, him will I confess also before my Father which is in heaven. **1 John 3:2** Beloved, now are we the sons of God, and it doth not yet appear what we shall be: but we know that, when he

shall appear, we shall be like him; for we shall see him as he is. **1 Cor. 13:12** For now we see through a glass, darkly; but then face to face: now I know in part; but then shall I know even as also I am known. **1 Thess. 4:17** Then we which are alive and remain shall be caught up together with them in the clouds, to meet the Lord in the air: and so shall we ever be with the Lord. **18** Wherefore comfort one another with these words. **2 Cor. 5:1** For we know that if our earthly house of this tabernacle were dissolved, we have a building of God, an house not made with hands, eternal in the heavens. **2** For in this we groan, earnestly desiring to be clothed upon with our house which is from heaven. **Phil. 1:21** For to me to live is Christ, and to die is gain. **22** But if I live in the flesh, this is the fruit of my labour: yet what I shall choose I wot not.

Luke 16:25 But Abraham said, Son, remember that thou in thy lifetime receivedst thy good things, and likewise Lazarus evil things: but now he is comforted, and thou art tormented. **1 Pet. 3:19** By which also he went and preached unto the spirits in prison; **20** Which sometime were disobedient, when once the longsuffering of God waited in the days of Noah, while the ark was a preparing, wherein few, that is, eight souls were saved by water.

Luke 16:23 And in hell he lift up his eyes, being in torments, and seeth Abraham afar off, and Lazarus in his bosom. **24** And he cried and said, Father Abraham, have mercy on me, and send Lazarus, that he may dip the tip of his finger in water, and cool my tongue; for I am tormented in this flame. **Acts 1:25** That he may take part of this ministry and apostleship, from which Judas by transgression fell, that he might go to his own place. **1 Pet. 3:19** By which also he went and preached unto the spirits in prison. **Ps. 49:11** Their inward thought is, that their houses shall continue for ever, and their dwelling places to all generations;

they call their lands after their own names. **John 9:28** Then they reviled him, and said, Thou art his disciple; but we are Moses' disciples. **29** We know that God spake unto Moses: as for this fellow, we know not from whence he is. **2 Thess. 1:8** In flaming fire taking vengeance on them that know not God, and that obey not the gospel of our Lord Jesus Christ: **9** Who shall be punished with everlasting destruction from the presence of the Lord, and from the glory of his power.

17. Of the Law

WE BELIEVE GOD requires obedience of man, and that the rule of that obedience is the moral law as it is in the hands of Christ; which teacheth all persons their duty to God, and to man; the sum of all being this, to love the Lord our God with all our hearts, with all our souls, and with all our strength, and our neighbours as ourselves. And that though the law is abolished as a covenant of works, and as so considered, we are dead to it, and that dead to us; yet it remains as a rule of life and righteousness for ever.

> **Mic. 6:8** He hath shewed thee, O man, what is good; and what doth the LORD require of thee, but to do justly, and to love mercy, and to walk humbly with thy God? **1 Sam. 15:22** And Samuel said, Hath the LORD as great delight in burnt offerings and sacrifices, as in obeying the voice of the LORD? Behold, to obey is better than sacrifice, and to hearken than the fat of rams. **Rev. 2:14** But I have a few things against thee, because thou hast there them that hold the doctrine of Balaam, who taught Balac to cast a stumblingblock before the children of Israel, to eat things sacrificed unto idols, and to commit fornication.

Matt. 19:17 And he said unto him, Why callest thou me good? there is none good but one, that is, God: but if thou wilt enter into life, keep the commandments. **Matt. 22:37** Jesus said unto him, Thou shalt love the Lord thy God with all thy heart, and with all thy soul, and with all thy mind. **38** This is the first and great commandment. **39** And the second is like unto it, Thou shalt love thy neighbour as thyself. **40** On these two commandments hang all the law and the prophets.

1 John 3:4 Whosoever committeth sin transgresseth also the law: for sin is the transgression of the law. **Rom. 7:3** So then if, while her husband liveth, she be married to another man, she shall be called an adulteress: but if her husband be dead, she is free from that law; so that she is no adulteress, though she be married to another man. **4** Wherefore, my brethren, ye also are become dead to the law by the body of Christ; that ye should be married to another, even to him who is raised from the dead, that we should bring forth fruit unto God.

18. We believe no mere man, since the fall, is able in this life perfectly to keep the holy law of God; and that every offence against the law deserves eternal death, though some sins are more heinous in God's sight than others.

Gen. 6:5 And GOD saw that the wickedness of man was great in the earth, and that every imagination of the thoughts of his heart was only evil continually. *****Rom. 3:9-20. Ezek. 8:6** He said furthermore unto me, Son of man, seest thou what they do? even the great abominations that the house of Israel committeth here, that I should go far off from my sanctuary? but turn thee yet again, and thou shalt see greater abominations.

1 John 5:16 If any man see his brother sin a sin which is not unto death, he shall ask, and he shall give him life for them that sin not unto death. There is a sin unto death: I do not say that he shall pray for it. **Ps. 78:17** And they sinned yet more against him by provoking the most High in the wilderness. **32** For all this they sinned still, and believed not for his wondrous works. **56** Yet they tempted and provoked the most high God, and kept not his testimonies.

And that God, as a simple act of mercy, will not, doth not, pardon any man; neither doth it seem consistent with his holiness and justice so to do, without a full satisfaction: wherefore he substituted Christ in our room and stead, perfectly to keep the whole law, and to die, or bear that wrath which we deserved for our breaking of it; he being pleased in his infinite love and grace to transfer our sins, guilt and punishment, upon his own Son (who took our nature upon him, as our blessed head and representative), that his active obedience and righteousness might be our just title unto eternal life; and his death (who bore our hell-torments) be our full discharge from the wrath of God, and eternal condemnation.

Exod. 34:6 And the LORD passed by before him, and proclaimed, The LORD, The LORD God, merciful and gracious, longsuffering, and abundant in goodness and truth.

Rom. 3:25 Whom God hath set forth to be a propitiation through faith in his blood, to declare his righteousness for the remission of sins that are past, through the forbearance of God; **26** To declare, I say, at this time his righteousness: that he might be just, and the justifier of him which believeth in Jesus.

Gal. 4:4 But when the fulness of the time was come, God sent forth his Son, made of a woman, made under the law.

A SHORT CONFESSION OF FAITH

Isa. 53:4 Surely he hath borne our griefs, and carried our sorrows: yet we did esteem him stricken, smitten of God, and afflicted. **5** But he was wounded for our transgressions, he was bruised for our iniquities: the chastisement of our peace was upon him; and with his stripes we are healed. **6** All we like sheep have gone astray; we have turned every one to his own way; and the LORD hath laid on him the iniquity of us all. **10** Yet it pleased the LORD to bruise him; he hath put him to grief: when thou shalt make his soul an offering for sin, he shall see his seed, he shall prolong his days, and the pleasure of the LORD shall prosper in his hand. **11** He shall see of the travail of his soul, and shall be satisfied: by his knowledge shall my righteous servant justify many; for he shall bear their iniquities. **1 Pet. 2:24** Who his own self bare our sins in his own body on the tree, that we, being dead to sins, should live unto righteousness: by whose stripes ye were healed.

Rom. 8:1 There is therefore now no condemnation to them which are in Christ Jesus, who walk not after the flesh, but after the Spirit.

And that all who would receive this title, and have this discharge so as to escape God's wrath, and the curse of the law, must fly to Christ, and lay hold on him by faith; which faith is known by its fruits, having lively, sin-killing, soul-humbling, self-abasing, Christ-exalting, and heart-purifying operations, always attending it.

John 5:24 Verily, verily, I say unto you, He that heareth my word, and believeth on him that sent me, hath everlasting life, and shall not come into condemnation; but is passed from death unto life. **John 3:15** That whosoever believeth in him should not perish, but have eternal life. **16** For God so loved the world, that he gave his only begotten Son, that whosoever believeth in him should not perish, but have everlasting life.

Heb. 6:18 That by two immutable things, in which it was impossible for God to lie, we might have a strong consolation, who have fled for refuge to lay hold upon the hope set before us: **19** Which hope we have as an anchor of the soul, both sure and stedfast, and which entereth into that within the veil; **20** Whither the forerunner is for us entered, even Jesus, made an high priest for ever after the order of Melchisedec. **Col. 2:12** Buried with him in baptism, wherein also ye are risen with him through the faith of the operation of God, who hath raised him from the dead. **Acts 15:9** And put no difference between us and them, purifying their hearts by faith. **Acts 2:36** Therefore let all the house of Israel know assuredly, that God hath made that same Jesus, whom ye have crucified, both Lord and Christ. **Job 42:5** I have heard of thee by the hearing of the ear: but now mine eye seeth thee. **1 Pet. 2:7** Unto you therefore which believe he is precious: but unto them which be disobedient, the stone which the builders disallowed, the same is made the head of the corner. **John 3:3** Jesus answered and said unto him, Verily, verily, I say unto thee, Except a man be born again, he cannot see the kingdom of God.

19. Of Faith and Repentance

WE BELIEVE THAT faith is a saving grace, or the most precious gift of God; and that it is an instrument whereby we receive, take hold of, and wholly rest upon Jesus Christ, as offered to us in the gospel. That repentance unto life is also a saving grace, whereby a sinner, out of a true sense of sin, and apprehension of God's mercy in Christ, doth with grief and hatred of his sins, turn from them. And that though repentance is in order of nature called the first principle of the doctrine of Christ, yet we believe no man can savingly repent, unless he believes in Jesus Christ, and apprehends the free pardon and forgiveness of all his sins through the blood of the everlasting covenant, and the sight and sense of God's love in a bleeding Saviour; being that only thing that melts and breaks the stony heart of a poor sinner, as the sight of a free pardon from a prince humbles the stout heart of a rebellious malefactor.

John 1:12 But as many as received him, to them gave he power to become the sons of God, even to them that believe on his name. **Isa. 26:3** Thou wilt keep him in perfect peace, whose mind is stayed on thee: because he trusteth in thee. **4** Trust ye in the Lord for ever: for in the Lord Jehovah is everlasting strength. **Phil. 3:9** And be found in him, not having mine own righteousness, which is of the law, but that which is through the faith of Christ, the righteousness which is of God by faith. **Eph. 2:8** For by grace are ye saved through faith; and that not of yourselves: it is the gift of God.

Acts 2:37 Now when they heard this, they were pricked in their heart, and said unto Peter and to the rest of the apostles, Men and brethren, what shall we do? **Joel 2:12** Therefore also now, saith the Lord, turn ye even to me with all your heart, and with fasting, and with weeping, and with mourning. **Jer. 3:22** Return, ye backsliding children, and I will heal your backslidings. Behold, we come unto thee; for thou art the Lord our God. **Jer. 31:18** I have surely heard Ephraim bemoaning himself thus; Thou hast chastised me, and I was chastised, as a bullock unaccustomed to the yoke: turn thou me, and I shall be turned; for thou art the Lord my God. **19** Surely after that I was turned, I repented; and after that I was instructed, I smote upon my thigh: I was ashamed, yea, even confounded, because I did bear the reproach of my youth. **Ezek. 36:31** Then shall ye remember your own evil ways, and your doings that were not good, and shall lothe yourselves in your own sight for your iniquities and for your abominations. **2 Cor. 7:10** For godly sorrow worketh repentance to salvation not to be repented of: but the sorrow of the world worketh death. **Isa. 1:16** Wash you, make you clean; put away the evil of your doings from before mine eyes; cease to do evil; 17 Learn to do well; seek judgment, relieve the oppressed, judge the fatherless, plead for the widow. **Heb. 6:1** Therefore leaving the principles of the doctrine of Christ, let us go on unto perfection; not laying again the foundation of repentance from dead works, and of faith toward God, 2 Of the doctrine of baptisms, and of laying on of hands, and of resurrection of the dead, and of eternal judgment.

Zech. 12:10 And I will pour upon the house of David, and upon the inhabitants of Jerusalem, the spirit of grace and of supplications: and they shall look upon me whom they have pierced, and they shall mourn for him, as one mourneth for his only son, and shall be in bitterness for him, as one that is in bitterness for his firstborn.

Acts 2:36 Therefore let all the house of Israel know assuredly, that God hath made that same Jesus, whom ye have crucified, both Lord and Christ.

20. *Of the Means of Grace*

WE BELIEVE THAT the outward and more ordinary means, whereby Christ communicates to us the benefits of redemption, are his holy ordinances, as prayer, the word of God, and preaching, with baptism, and the Lord's supper, etc., and yet notwithstanding it is the Spirit of God that maketh prayer, reading, etc., and specially the preaching of the word, effectual to the convincing, converting, building up, and comforting, through faith, all the elect of God unto salvation.

Matt. 28:19 Go ye therefore, and teach all nations, baptizing them in the name of the Father, and of the Son, and of the Holy Ghost: **20** Teaching them to observe all things whatsoever I have commanded you: and, lo, I am with you alway, even unto the end of the world. Amen. **Acts 2:42** And they continued stedfastly in the apostles' doctrine and fellowship, and in breaking of bread, and in prayers. **46** And they, continuing daily with one accord in the temple, and breaking bread from house to house, did eat their meat with gladness and singleness of heart, **47** Praising God, and having favour with all the people. And the Lord added to the church daily such as should be saved. **Neh. 8:8** So they read in the book in the law of God distinctly, and gave the sense, and caused them to understand the reading. **1 Cor. 14:24** But if all prophesy, and there come in one that believeth not, or one unlearned, he is convinced of all, he is judged of all: **25** And thus are the secrets of his heart made manifest; and so falling down on his face he will worship God, and report that God is in you of a truth.

***Acts 20:32** And now, brethren, I commend you to God, and to the word of his grace, which is able to build you up, and to give you an inheritance among all them which are sanctified. **Ps. 19:8** The statutes of the LORD are right, rejoicing the heart: the commandment of the LORD is pure, enlightening the eyes. **Rom. 1:15** So, as much as in me is, I am ready to preach the gospel to you that are at Rome also. **16** For I am not ashamed of the gospel of Christ: for it is the power of God unto salvation to every one that believeth; to the Jew first, and also to the Greek.

And that it is the duty of all, that the word may become effectual to their salvation, to attend upon it with all diligence, preparation, and prayer, that they may receive it with faith and love, and lay it up in their hearts, and practise it in their lives.

> **Acts 20:32** And now, brethren, I commend you to God, and to the word of his grace, which is able to build you up, and to give you an inheritance among all them which are sanctified. **Rom. 10:13** For whosoever shall call upon the name of the Lord shall be saved. **14** How then shall they call on him in whom they have not believed? and how shall they believe in him of whom they have not heard? and how shall they hear without a preacher? **15** And how shall they preach, except they be sent? as it is written, How beautiful are the feet of them that preach the gospel of peace, and bring glad tidings of good things! **16** But they have not all obeyed the gospel. For Esaias saith, Lord, who hath believed our report? **17** So then faith cometh by hearing, and hearing by the word of God. **Prov. 8:34** Blessed is the man that heareth me, watching daily at my gates, waiting at the posts of my doors. **1 Pet. 2:1** Wherefore laying aside all malice, and all guile, and hypocrisies, and envies, and all evil speakings, **2** As newborn babes, desire the sincere milk of the word, that ye may grow thereby. **Ps. 119:18** Open thou mine eyes, that I may behold wondrous things out of thy law. **Heb. 4:2** For unto us was the gospel preached, as well as unto them: but the word preached did not profit them, not being mixed with faith in them that heard it. **2 Thess. 2:10** And with all deceivableness of unrighteousness in them that perish; because they received not the love of the truth, that they might be saved. **Jas. 1:25** But whoso looketh into the perfect law of liberty,

and continueth therein, he being not a forgetful hearer, but a doer of the work, this man shall be blessed in his deed.

21. Of Baptism

WE BELIEVE THAT baptism is a holy ordinance of Christ, or a pure gospel-institution; and to be unto the party baptized, a sign of his fellowship with Christ in his death, burial, and resurrection, and of his being grafted into him, and of remission of sins, and of his giving himself up to God, through Jesus Christ, to walk in newness of life.

> **1 Pet. 3:21** The like figure whereunto even baptism doth also now save us (not the putting away of the filth of the flesh, but the answer of a good conscience toward God,) by the resurrection of Jesus Christ. **1 Cor. 12:13** For by one Spirit are we all baptized into one body, whether we be Jews or Gentiles, whether we be bond or free; and have been all made to drink into one Spirit. **Matt. 28:19** Go ye therefore, and teach all nations, baptizing them in the name of the Father, and of the Son, and of the Holy Ghost: **20** Teaching them to observe all things whatsoever I have commanded you: and, lo, I am with you alway, even unto the end of the world. Amen. **Rom. 6:3** Know ye not, that so many of us as were baptized into Jesus Christ were baptized into his death? **4** Therefore we are buried with him by baptism into death: that like as Christ was raised up from the dead by the glory of the Father, even so we also should walk in newness of life. **5** For if we have been planted together in the likeness of his death, we shall be also in the likeness of his resurrection. **Col. 2:12** Buried with him in baptism, wherein also ye are risen with him through the faith of the operation of God, who hath raised

him from the dead. 13 And you, being dead in your sins and the uncircumcision of your flesh, hath he quickened together with him, having forgiven you all trespasses. **Gal. 3:27** For as many of you as have been baptized into Christ have put on Christ. **Acts 2:38** Then Peter said unto them, Repent, and be baptized every one of you in the name of Jesus Christ for the remission of sins, and ye shall receive the gift of the Holy Ghost. **Acts 22:16** And now why tarriest thou? arise, and be baptized, and wash away thy sins, calling on the name of the Lord.

We also believe that baptism ought not to be administered to any but to those who actually profess repentance towards God, and faith towards our Lord Jesus Christ.

Acts 8:37 And Philip said, If thou believest with all thine heart, thou mayest. And he answered and said, I believe that Jesus Christ is the Son of God. *****Col. 2:11** In whom also ye are circumcised with the circumcision made without hands, in putting off the body of the sins of the flesh by the circumcision of Christ: *12 Buried with him in baptism, wherein also ye are risen with him through the faith of the operation of God, who hath raised him from the dead.

That the infants of believers ought not to be baptized, because there is neither precept, or example, or any certain consequence in the holy Scripture for any such practice: And we ought not to be wise above what is written. And that a human tradition or custom ought not to be regarded, but that it is sinful, and abominable.

Rev. 22:18 For I testify unto every man that heareth the words of the prophecy of this book, If any man shall add unto these things, God shall add unto him the plagues that are written in this book. **Prov. 30:6** Add thou not unto his words, lest he reprove thee, and thou be found a liar.

We believe also that baptism is only rightly administered by immersion, or dipping the whole body in water, into the Name of the Father, and of the Son, and of the Holy Spirit; according to Christ's institution, and the practice of the Apostles; and not by sprinkling, or pouring of water, or dipping some part of the body in water, after the tradition of men.

Matt. 28:19 Go ye therefore, and teach all nations, baptizing them in the name of the Father, and of the Son, and of the Holy Ghost: **20** Teaching them to observe all things whatsoever I have commanded you: and, lo, I am with you alway, even unto the end of the world. Amen. **Matt. 3:16** And Jesus, when he was baptized, went up straightway out of the water: and, lo, the heavens were opened unto him, and he saw the Spirit of God descending like a dove, and lighting upon him. **John 3:23** And John also was baptizing in Aenon near to Salim, because there was much water there: and they came, and were baptized. **Acts 8:38** And he commanded the chariot to stand still: and they went down both into the water, both Philip and the eunuch; and he baptized him. **Rom. 6:3** Know ye not, that so many of us as were baptized into Jesus Christ were baptized into his death? *__**Col. 2:12**__ Buried with him in baptism, wherein also ye are risen with him through the faith of the operation of God, who hath raised him from the dead.

And that it is the indispensable duty of such who are baptized, to give up themselves to some particular orderly church of Jesus Christ, and to walk in all the commandments and ordinances of the Lord blameless: Baptism being an initiating ordinance.

> **Acts 2:41** Then they that gladly received his word were baptized: and the same day there were added unto them about three thousand souls. **42** And they continued stedfastly in the apostles' doctrine and fellowship, and in breaking of bread, and in prayers. **Acts 5:13** And of the rest durst no man join himself to them: but the people magnified them. **14** And believers were the more added to the Lord, multitudes both of men and women. **1 Pet. 2:5** Ye also, as lively stones, are built up a spiritual house, an holy priesthood, to offer up spiritual sacrifices, acceptable to God by Jesus Christ. **Luke 1:6** And they were both righteous before God, walking in all the commandments and ordinances of the Lord blameless.

22. *Of a True Church*

WE BELIEVE A true church of Christ is not national, nor parochial, but doth consist of a number of godly persons, who upon the profession of their faith and repentance have been baptized, and in a solemn manner have in a holy covenant given themselves up to the Lord, and to one another, to live in love, and to endeavour to keep the unity of the Spirit in the bond of peace: Among whom the word of God is duly and truly preached; and holy baptism, the Lord's supper, and all other ordinances are duly administered, according to the word of God, and the institution of Christ in the Primitive Church: watching over one another, and communicating to each other's necessities, as becometh saints; living holy lives, as becomes their sacred profession; and not to forsake the assembling themselves, as the manner of some is; or to take leave to hear where they please in other places when the church is assembled, but to worship God, and feed in that pasture, or with that church, with whom they have covenanted, and given up themselves as particular members thereof.

> **Acts 2:40** And with many other words did he testify and exhort, saying, Save yourselves from this untoward generation. 41 Then they that gladly received his word were baptized: and the same day there were added unto them about three thousand souls. 42 And they continued stedfastly in the apostles' doctrine and fellowship, and in breaking of bread, and in prayers.
>
> **Eph. 4:3** Endeavouring to keep the unity of the Spirit in the bond of peace.
>
> ***Acts 2:40-47. 1 Cor. 16:1** Now concerning the collection for the saints, as I have given order to the churches of Galatia, even so do ye. 2 Upon the first day of the week let every one of you lay by him in store, as God hath prospered him, that there be no gatherings when I come.
>
> **Heb. 10:25** Not forsaking the assembling of ourselves together, as the manner of some is; but exhorting one another: and so much the more, as ye see the day approaching.

23. *Of Laying on of Hands*

We believe that laying on of hands (with prayer) upon baptized believers, as such, is an ordinance of Christ, and ought to be submitted unto by all such persons that are admitted to partake of the Lord's supper; and that the end of this ordinance is not for the extraordinary gifts of the Spirit, but for a farther reception of the Holy Spirit of promise, or for the addition of the graces of the Spirit, and the influences thereof; to confirm, strengthen, and comfort them in Christ Jesus; it being ratified and established by the extraordinary gifts of the Spirit in the primitive times, to abide in the Church, as meeting together on the first day of the week was (Acts 2:1), that being the day of worship, or Christian Sabbath, under the gospel; and as preaching the word was (Acts 10:44), and as baptism was (Matt. 3:16), and prayer was (Acts 4:31), and singing Psalms, etc., was (Acts 16:25–26), so this of laying on of hands was (Acts 8, 19). For as the whole gospel was confirmed by signs and wonders, and divers miracles and gifts of the Holy Ghost in general, so was every ordinance in like manner confirmed in particular.

> **Heb. 5:12** For when for the time ye ought to be teachers, ye have need that one teach you again which be the first principles of the oracles of God; and are become such as have need of milk, and not of strong meat. **Heb. 6:1** Therefore leaving the principles of the doctrine of Christ, let us go on unto perfection; not laying again the foundation of repentance from dead works, and of faith toward God, **2** Of the doctrine of baptisms, and of laying on of hands, and of resurrection of the dead, and of eternal judgment. **Acts 8. Acts 19:6** And when Paul had laid his hands upon them, the Holy Ghost came on them; and they spake with tongues, and prophesied.
>
> **Eph. 1:13** In whom ye also trusted, after that ye heard the word of truth, the gospel of your salvation: in whom also after that ye believed, ye were sealed with that holy Spirit of promise, **14** Which is the earnest of our inheritance until the redemption of the purchased possession, unto the praise of his glory.

Acts 8. Acts 19:6 And when Paul had laid his hands upon them, the Holy Ghost came on them; and they spake with tongues, and prophesied.

Acts 2:1 And when the day of Pentecost was fully come, they were all with one accord in one place. **Acts 10:44** While Peter yet spake these words, the Holy Ghost fell on all them which heard the word. **Matt. 3:16** And Jesus, when he was baptized, went up straightway out of the water: and, lo, the heavens were opened unto him, and he saw the Spirit of God descending like a dove, and lighting upon him. **Acts 4:31** And when they had prayed, the place was shaken where they were assembled together; and they were all filled with the Holy Ghost, and they spake the word of God with boldness. **Acts 16:25** And at midnight Paul and Silas prayed, and sang praises unto God: and the prisoners heard them. **26** And suddenly there was a great earthquake, so that the foundations of the prison were shaken: and immediately all the doors were opened, and every one's bands were loosed. **Acts 8. Acts 19.**

Heb. 2:3 How shall we escape, if we neglect so great salvation; which at the first began to be spoken by the Lord, and was confirmed unto us by them that heard him; **4** God also bearing them witness, both with signs and wonders, and with divers miracles, and gifts of the Holy Ghost, according to his own will?

24. *Of the Lord's Supper*

WE BELIEVE THAT the holy ordinance of the Lord's supper, which he instituted the night before he was betrayed, ought to be observed to the end of the world; and that it consisteth only in breaking of bread, and drinking of wine, in remembrance of Christ's death; it being appointed for our spiritual nourishment, and growth in grace, and as a farther engagement in, and to all duties we owe to Jesus Christ, and as a pledge of his eternal love to us, and as a token of our communion with him, and one with another. And that due preparation and examination is required of all that ought to partake thereof; and that it cannot be neglected by any approved and orderly member without sin.

> **Matt. 26:26** And as they were eating, Jesus took bread, and blessed it, and brake it, and gave it to the disciples, and said, Take, eat; this is my body. **27** And he took the cup, and gave thanks, and gave it to them, saying, Drink ye all of it; **28** For this is my blood of the new testament, which is shed for many for the remission of sins. **Mark 14:21** The Son of man indeed goeth, as it is written of him: but woe to that man by whom the Son of man is betrayed! good were it for that man if he had never been born. **22** And as they did eat, Jesus took bread, and blessed, and brake it, and gave to them, and said, Take, eat: this is my body. **23** And he took the cup, and when he had given thanks, he gave it to them: and they all drank of it. **Luke 22:19** And he took bread, and gave thanks, and brake it, and gave unto them, saying, This is my body which is given for you: this do in remembrance of me. **20** Likewise also the cup after supper, saying, This cup is the new testament in my blood, which is shed for you. **1 Cor. 11:23** For I have received of the Lord that which also I delivered unto you, That the Lord Jesus the same night in which he was betrayed took bread: **24** And when he had given thanks, he brake it, and said, Take, eat: this is my body, which is broken for you: this do in remembrance of me. **25** After the same manner also he took the cup, when he had supped, saying, This cup is the

new testament in my blood: this do ye, as oft as ye drink it, in remembrance of me. **26** For as often as ye eat this bread, and drink this cup, ye do shew the Lord's death till he come. **27** Wherefore whosoever shall eat this bread, and drink this cup of the Lord, unworthily, shall be guilty of the body and blood of the Lord. *****Acts 20:7** And upon the first day of the week, when the disciples came together to break bread, Paul preached unto them, ready to depart on the morrow; and continued his speech until midnight.

25. Of Church Officers

WE DO BELIEVE that every particular church of Christ is independent; and that no one church hath any priority or super-intendency above or over another: and that every church ought to be organical: that an elder, or elders, a deacon, or deacons, ought to be elected in every congregation, according to those holy qualifications laid down in the word of God: and that the said elders and deacons so chosen, ought solemnly to be ordained with prayer, and laying on of hands of the eldership. That such churches as have not officers so ordained, are disorderly, there being something still wanting.

*****1 Tim. 3. Titus 1:5** For this cause left I thee in Crete, that thou shouldest set in order the things that are wanting, and ordain elders in every city, as I had appointed thee.

1 Tim. 3:2–12. Titus 1:5 For this cause left I thee in Crete, that thou shouldest set in order the things that are wanting, and ordain elders in every city, as I had appointed thee: **6** If any be blameless, the husband of one wife, having faithful children not accused of riot or unruly. 7 For a bishop must be blameless, as the steward of God; not selfwilled, not soon angry, not given to wine, no striker, not given to filthy lucre; 8 But a lover of hospitality, a lover of good men, sober, just, holy, temperate. **Acts 13:3** And when they had fasted and prayed, and laid their hands on them, they sent them away. **1 Tim. 5:22** Lay hands suddenly on no man, neither be partaker of other men's sins: keep thyself pure. **1 Tim. 4:14** Neglect not the gift that is in thee, which was given thee by prophecy, with the laying on of the hands of the presbytery.

26. Of Prayer

WE BELIEVE PRAYER is a holy ordinance of God, and that it ought to be performed by the help and assistance of the Holy Spirit; and that not only the prayer Christ taught his disciples, but the whole word of God is to be our rule how to pray, and pour forth our souls unto God: and that it is the indispensable duty of all godly families (and others also) as well as private Christians, daily to pray for all things they need, and to give thanks every day for all good things they receive: and that the omission of this duty is a great scandal to religion, and a great evil when it is carelessly or negligently performed.

Phil. 4:6 Be careful for nothing; but in every thing by prayer and supplication with thanksgiving let your requests be made known unto God. **Ps. 65:2** O thou that hearest prayer, unto thee shall all flesh come. **John 4:23** But the hour cometh, and now is, when the true worshippers shall worship the Father in spirit and in truth: for the Father seeketh such to worship him. **1 Pet. 2:5** Ye also, as lively stones, are built up a spiritual house, an holy priesthood, to offer up spiritual sacrifices, acceptable to God by Jesus Christ. **Rom. 8:26** Likewise the Spirit also helpeth our infirmities: for we know not what we should pray for as we ought: but the Spirit itself maketh intercession for us with groanings which cannot be uttered. *__1 John 5:14__ And this is the confidence that we have in him, that, if we ask any thing according to his will, he heareth us. **Ps. 47:7** For God is the King of all the earth: sing ye praises with understanding. **Eccl. 5:1** Keep thy foot when thou goest to the house of God, and be more ready to hear, than to give the sacrifice of fools: for they consider not that they do evil. **2** Be not rash with thy mouth, and let not thine heart be hasty to utter any thing before God: for God is in heaven, and thou upon earth: therefore let thy words be few. **Jas. 5:16** Confess your faults one to another, and pray one for another, that ye may be healed. The effectual fervent prayer of a righteous man availeth much. **Eph. 6:18** Praying always with all prayer and supplication in the Spirit, and watching thereunto with all perseverance and supplication for all saints. **1 Cor. 14:14** For if I pray in an unknown tongue, my spirit prayeth, but my understanding is unfruitful. **Col. 4:2** Continue in prayer, and watch in the same with thanksgiving. **Josh. 24:15** And if it seem evil unto you to serve the Lord, choose you this day whom ye will serve; whether the gods which your fathers served that were on the other side of the flood, or the gods of the Amorites, in whose land ye dwell: but as for me and my house, we will serve the Lord. **Gen. 18:19** For I know him, that he will command his children and his household after him, and they shall keep the way of the Lord, to do justice and judgment; that the Lord may bring upon Abraham that which he hath spoken of him.

Jer. 10:25 Pour out thy fury upon the heathen that know thee not, and upon the families that call not on thy name: for they have eaten up Jacob, and devoured him, and consumed him, and have made his habitation desolate.

27. Of Singing of Psalms, etc.

WE BELIEVE THAT singing the praises of God, is a holy ordinance of Christ, and not a part of natural religion, or a moral duty only; but that it is brought under divine institution, it being enjoined on the churches of Christ to sing psalms, hymns, and spiritual songs; and that the whole church in their public assemblies (as well as private Christians) ought to sing God's praises, according to the best light they have received. Moreover, it was practised in the great representative church, by our Lord Jesus Christ with his disciples, after he had instituted and celebrated the sacred ordinance of his holy supper, as a commemorative token of redeeming love.

Eph. 5:19 Speaking to yourselves in psalms and hymns and spiritual songs, singing and making melody in your heart to the Lord. Col. 3:16 Let the word of Christ dwell in you richly in all wisdom; teaching and admonishing one another in psalms and hymns and spiritual songs, singing with grace in your hearts to the Lord.

Acts 16:25 And at midnight Paul and Silas prayed, and sang praises unto God: and the prisoners heard them. Heb. 2:12 Saying, I will declare thy name unto my brethren, in the midst of the church will I sing praise unto thee. Jas. 5:13 Is any among you afflicted? let him pray. Is any merry? let him sing psalms.

Matt. 26:30 And when they had sung an hymn, they went out into the mount of Olives. **Mark 14:26** And when they had sung an hymn, they went out into the mount of Olives.

28. Of the Christian Sabbath

WE BELIEVE THAT one day in seven, ought to be solemnly observed in the worship of God; and that by Moses' Law the Jews and proselyted strangers were to keep the seventh day: but from the resurrection of Christ the first day of the week ought by all Christians to be observed holy to the Lord, that being called the Lord's day; and the first time the Church met together after Christ's ascension was on the day of Pentecost, which was the first day of the week, as tradition hath handed it down: and on that day the Church also met together to break bread, and make collections for the poor saints: and no mention is made that any one gospel church kept the Jewish Sabbath in all the New Testament. And we believe that an apostolical precedent is equivalent to an apostolical precept in this case.

***Exod. 20:8** Remember the sabbath day, to keep it holy. **9** Six days shalt thou labour, and do all thy work: **10** But the seventh day is the sabbath of the LORD thy God: in it thou shalt not do any work, thou, nor thy son, nor thy daughter, thy manservant, nor thy maidservant, nor thy cattle, nor thy stranger that is within thy gates: **11** For in six days the LORD made heaven and earth, the sea, and all that in them is, and rested the seventh day: wherefore the LORD blessed the sabbath day, and hallowed it.

Rev. 1:10 I was in the Spirit on the Lord's day, and heard behind me a great voice, as of a trumpet.

Acts 2:1 And when the day of Pentecost was fully come, they were all with one accord in one place. 2 And suddenly there came a sound from heaven as of a rushing mighty wind, and it filled all the house where they were sitting. **Acts 20:7** And upon the first day of the week, when the disciples came together to break bread, Paul preached unto them, ready to depart on the morrow; and continued his speech until midnight.

1 Cor. 16:2 Upon the first day of the week let every one of you lay by him in store, as God hath prospered him, that there be no gatherings when I come.

29. Of Ministers, and their Maintenance

WE DO BELIEVE that every brother that hath received a gift to preach, having first passed the probation of the church, and being regularly called by the same, ought to exercise the said gift to the edification of the church when desired; and that no brother ought to take upon him to preach, until he has a lawful call so to do.

1 **Tim. 3:2** A bishop then must be blameless, the husband of one wife, vigilant, sober, of good behaviour, given to hospitality, apt to teach. **Eph. 4:11** And he gave some, apostles; and some, prophets; and some, evangelists; and some, pastors and teachers.

1 **Pet. 4:10** As every man hath received the gift, even so minister the same one to another, as good stewards of the manifold grace of God. **Rom. 12:6** Having then gifts differing according

to the grace that is given to us, whether prophecy, let us prophesy according to the proportion of faith; 7 Or ministry, let us wait on our ministering: or he that teacheth, on teaching.

Moreover, we believe that it is the indispensable duty of every church, according to their ability, to provide their pastor, or elders, a comfortable maintenance; as God hath ordained, that he that preaches the gospel, should live of the gospel, and not of his own labour; but that he should wholly give himself up to the work of the ministry, and to watch over the flock, being to be freed from all secular business, and encumbrances of the world: and yet that it is abominable evil for any man to preach the gospel for filthy lucre sake, but he must do it of a ready mind.

1 Cor. 9:9–14. Rom. 15:27 It hath pleased them verily; and their debtors they are. For if the Gentiles have been made partakers of their spiritual things, their duty is also to minister unto them in carnal things. **Gal. 6:6** Let him that is taught in the word communicate unto him that teacheth in all good things. **1 Tim. 5:15** For some are already turned aside after Satan.

1 Pet. 5:2 Feed the flock of God which is among you, taking the oversight thereof, not by constraint, but willingly; not for filthy lucre, but of a ready mind.

30. Of the First Covenant

WE BELIEVE THAT the first covenant, or covenant of works, was primarily made with Adam, and with all mankind in him, by virtue of which he stood in a justified state before the fall, upon the condition of his own perfect and personal obedience. But by the fall he made himself incapable of life by that covenant.

> **Gen. 2:17** But of the tree of the knowledge of good and evil, thou shalt not eat of it: for in the day that thou eatest thereof thou shalt surely die.
> **Rom. 3:12** They are all gone out of the way, they are together become unprofitable; there is none that doeth good, no, not one.
> **Rom. 10:5** For Moses describeth the righteousness which is of the law, That the man which doeth those things shall live by them. **Rom. 5:10–20.**

That the law God gave by Moses to Israel, was of the same nature of that given to Adam, being a second ministration of it; but not given for life, but to make sin exceeding sinful, and to show how unable man was in his fallen state to fulfil the righteousness of God; and so (with the ceremonial law) it was given in subserviency to the gospel, as a schoolmaster to bring sinners to Christ.

> **Rom. 3:19** Now we know that what things soever the law saith, it saith to them who are under the law: that every mouth may be stopped, and all the world may become guilty before God. 20 Therefore by the deeds of the law there shall no flesh be justified in his sight: for by the law is the knowledge of sin.
> **2 Cor. 3:9** For if the ministration of condemnation be glory, much more doth the ministration of righteousness exceed in glory. 11 For if that which is done away was glorious, much more that which remaineth is glorious.
> **Rom. 7:7–13.**

*****Gal. 3:24** Wherefore the law was our schoolmaster to bring us unto Christ, that we might be justified by faith.

31. Of the New and Second Covenant

WE BELIEVE THE covenant of grace was primarily made with the second Adam, and in him with all the elect, who as God-man, or Mediator, was set up from everlasting as a common person, or as their head and representative; who freely obliged or engaged himself to the Father for them, perfectly to keep the whole law in their nature that had sinned, and to satisfy divine justice by bearing their sins upon his own body, i.e. the guilt of all their sins, which were laid upon him: and that he sustained that wrath and curse in his body and soul, that was due to them for all their transgressions: and having received their discharge from wrath and condemnation, he gives it out to all that believe in him, and obtain union with him, who are thereby brought actually into the said new covenant, and have a personal right to all the blessings thereof.

Zech. 6:13 Even he shall build the temple of the LORD; and he shall bear the glory, and shall sit and rule upon his throne; and he shall be a priest upon his throne: and the counsel of peace shall be between them both.

Rom. 3:23 For all have sinned, and come short of the glory of God; **24** Being justified freely by his grace through the redemption that is in Christ Jesus: **25** Whom God hath set forth to be a propitiation through faith in his blood, to declare his righteousness for the remission of sins that are past, through the forbearance of God; 26 To declare, I say, at this time his righteousness: that he might be just, and the justifier of him which believeth in Jesus. *Isa. 53:5 But he was wounded for our transgressions, he was bruised for our iniquities: the chastisement of our peace was upon him; and with his stripes we are healed. 6 All we like sheep have gone astray; we have turned every one to his own way; and the Lord hath laid on him the iniquity of us all. 10 Yet it pleased the Lord to bruise him; he hath put him to grief: when thou shalt make his soul an offering for sin, he shall see his seed, he shall prolong his days, and the pleasure of the Lord shall prosper in his hand. 11 He shall see of the travail of his soul, and shall be satisfied: by his knowledge shall my righteous servant justify many; for he shall bear their iniquities.

Rom. 8:3 For what the law could not do, in that it was weak through the flesh, God sending his own Son in the likeness of sinful flesh, and for sin, condemned sin in the flesh. **Heb. 9:15** And for this cause he is the mediator of the new testament, that by means of death, for the redemption of the transgressions that were under the first testament, they which are called might receive the promise of eternal inheritance. **16** For where a testament is, there must also of necessity be the death of the testator. **17** For a testament is of force after men are dead: otherwise it is of no strength at all while the testator liveth.

Heb. 7:22 By so much was Jesus made a surety of a better testament.

Luke 22:20 Likewise also the cup after supper, saying, This cup is the new testament in my blood, which is shed for you.

1 Cor. 11:25 After the same manner also he took the cup, when he had supped, saying, This cup is the new testament in my blood: this do ye, as oft as ye drink it, in remembrance of me.

Rom. 6:21 What fruit had ye then in those things whereof ye are now ashamed? for the end of those things is death. **Rom. 8:16** The Spirit itself beareth witness with our spirit, that we are the children of God: **17** And if children, then heirs; heirs of God, and joint-heirs with Christ; if so be that we suffer with him, that we may be also glorified together. **18** For I reckon that the sufferings of this present time are not worthy to be compared with the glory which shall be revealed in us.

32. Of Election

WE DO BELIEVE that God from all eternity, according unto the most wise and holy counsel of his own will, freely and unchangeably decreed and ordained, for the manifestation of his own glory, some angels, and some of the lost sons and daughters of Adam, unto eternal life; and that their number is so certain and definite, that it cannot be either increased or diminished: and that others are left or passed by under a decree of preterition. And that those of mankind that are predestinated and fore-ordained, are particularly and personally designed unto eternal life: and these God, according to his eternal and immutable purpose, and good pleasure of his will, did choose in Christ (the head of this election) unto everlasting glory, of his mere free grace, without any foreseen faith or obedience and perseverance therein, or any thing in the creature as a condition or cause moving him thereunto; and all this only to the praise of his own glorious grace.

Rom. 8:29 For whom he did foreknow, he also did predestinate to be conformed to the image of his Son, that he might be the firstborn among many brethren. **30** Moreover whom he did predestinate, them he also called: and whom he called, them he also justified: and whom he justified, them he also glorified. 31 What shall we then say to these things? If God be for us, who can be against us?

Acts 13:48 And when the Gentiles heard this, they were glad, and glorified the word of the Lord: and as many as were ordained to eternal life believed.

Rom. 9:11 For the children being not yet born, neither having done any good or evil, that the purpose of God according to election might stand, not of works, but of him that calleth.

*****1 Thess. 1:4** Knowing, brethren beloved, your election of God. 5 For our gospel came not unto you in word only, but also in power, and in the Holy Ghost, and in much assurance; as ye know what manner of men we were among you for your sake.

Eph. 1:3 Blessed be the God and Father of our Lord Jesus Christ, who hath blessed us with all spiritual blessings in heavenly places in Christ: 4 According as he hath chosen us in him before the foundation of the world, that we should be holy and without blame before him in love. 11 In whom also we have obtained an inheritance, being predestinated according to the purpose of him who worketh all things after the counsel of his own will.

2 Thess. 2:13 But we are bound to give thanks alway to God for you, brethren beloved of the Lord, because God hath from the beginning chosen you to salvation through sanctification of the Spirit and belief of the truth.

33. Of Final Perseverance

WE BELIEVE ALL those whom God hath chosen, and who are effectually called, justified, and sanctified in

Jesus Christ, can neither totally, nor finally fall away from a state of grace; but shall certainly persevere therein unto the end, and eternally be saved; and this by virtue of their election, or the immutable decree of God, and the unchangeable love of God the Father; and by virtue of their union with Christ, together with his death, resurrection, and intercession; as also from the nature of the covenant of grace, and suretyship of Christ; and through the indwelling of the Holy Spirit, who abideth in them for ever.

> **Rom. 8:28** And we know that all things work together for good to them that love God, to them who are the called according to his purpose. **29** For whom he did foreknow, he also did predestinate to be conformed to the image of his Son, that he might be the firstborn among many brethren. **30** Moreover whom he did predestinate, them he also called: and whom he called, them he also justified: and whom he justified, them he also glorified. **31** What shall we then say to these things? If God be for us, who can be against us?
>
> **John 10:28** And I give unto them eternal life; and they shall never perish, neither shall any man pluck them out of my hand. **29** My Father, which gave them me, is greater than all; and no man is able to pluck them out of my Father's hand. **Rom. 8:38** For I am persuaded, that neither death, nor life, nor angels, nor principalities, nor powers, nor things present, nor things to come, **39** Nor height, nor depth, nor any other creature, shall be able to separate us from the love of God, which is in Christ Jesus our Lord. **Rom. 8:32** He that spared not his own Son, but delivered him up for us all, how shall he not with him also freely give us all things? **33** Who shall lay any thing to the charge of God's elect? It is God that justifieth. **34** Who is he that condemneth? It is Christ that died,

yea rather, that is risen again, who is even at the right hand of God, who also maketh intercession for us.

2 Tim. 2:3 Thou therefore endure hardness, as a good soldier of Jesus Christ. 5 And if a man also strive for masteries, yet is he not crowned, except he strive lawfully.

2 Cor. 6:17 Wherefore come out from among them, and be ye separate, saith the Lord, and touch not the unclean thing; and I will receive you.

34. Of the Resurrection

WE BELIEVE THAT the bodies of all men, both the just and unjust, shall rise again at the last day, even the same numerical bodies that die; though the bodies of the saints shall be raised immortal and incorruptible, and be made like Christ's glorious body: and that the dead in Christ shall rise first.

35. Of Eternal Judgment

WE BELIEVE THAT God hath appointed a day in which he will judge the world in righteousness by Jesus Christ, or that there shall be a general day of judgment, when all shall stand before the judgment seat of Christ, and give an account to him for all things done in this body: and that he will pass an eternal sentence upon all, according as their works shall be.

Acts 17:31 Because he hath appointed a day, in the which he will judge the world in righteousness by that man whom he hath ordained; whereof he hath given assurance unto all men, in that he hath raised him from the dead.

2 Cor. 5:10 For we must all appear before the judgment seat of Christ; that every one may receive the things done in his body, according to that he hath done, whether it be good or bad.

Eccl. 12.

36. Of Marriage

WE BELIEVE MARRIAGE is God's holy ordinance, that is to say between one man and one woman: and that no man ought to have more than one wife at once: and that believers that marry, should marry in the Lord, or such that are believers, or godly persons; and that those who do otherwise, sin greatly, in violating God's holy precept: and that ministers as well as others may marry; for marriage is honourable in all.

***Gen. 2:24** Therefore shall a man leave his father and his mother, and shall cleave unto his wife: and they shall be one flesh.

Matt. 19:5 And said, For this cause shall a man leave father and mother, and shall cleave to his wife: and they twain shall be one flesh.

1 Cor. 6:16 What? know ye not that he which is joined to an harlot is one body? for two, saith he, shall be one flesh.

Eph. 5:31 For this cause shall a man leave his father and mother, and shall be joined unto his wife, and they two shall be one flesh.

Rom. 7:4 Wherefore, my brethren, ye also are become dead to the law by the body of Christ; that ye should be married to another, even to him who is raised from the dead, that we should bring forth fruit unto God.

Heb. 13:4 Marriage is honourable in all, and the bed undefiled: but whoremongers and adulterers God will judge.

37. Of Civil Magistrates

WE DO BELIEVE the supreme Lord of heaven and earth hath ordained magistrates for the good of mankind: and that it is our duty in all civil and lawful things to obey them for conscience' sake; nay, and to pray for all that are in authority, that under them we may live a godly and peaceable life: and that we ought to render unto Caesar the things that are Caesar's, and to God the things that are God's.

Rom. 13:1 Let every soul be subject unto the higher powers. For there is no power but of God: the powers that be are ordained of God. 2 Whosoever therefore resisteth the power, resisteth the ordinance of God: and they that resist shall receive to themselves damnation. 3 For rulers are not a terror to good works, but to the evil. Wilt thou then not be afraid of the power? do that which is good, and thou shalt have praise of the same.

Titus 3:1 Put them in mind to be subject to principalities and powers, to obey magistrates, to be ready to every good work.

1 Pet. 2:13 Submit yourselves to every ordinance of man for the Lord's sake: whether it be to the king, as supreme.

Matt. 22:21 They say unto him, Caesar's. Then saith he unto them, Render therefore unto Caesar the things which are Caesar's; and unto God the things that are God's.

38. Of Lawful Oaths

WE DO BELIEVE it is lawful to take some oaths before the civil magistrate; an oath of confirmation being to put an end to all strife: nay, and that it is our duty so to do when lawfully called thereunto: and that those that swear, ought to swear in truth, in righteousness, and in judgment.

Exod. 20:7 Thou shalt not take the name of the LORD thy God in vain; for the LORD will not hold him guiltless that taketh his name in vain.
Jer. 4:2 And thou shalt swear, The LORD liveth, in truth, in judgment, and in righteousness; and the nations shall bless themselves in him, and in him shall they glory. **Gen. 24:2** And Abraham said unto his eldest servant of his house, that ruled over all that he had, Put, I pray thee, thy hand under my thigh. **Neh. 5:12** Then said they, We will restore them, and will require nothing of them; so will we do as thou sayest. Then I called the priests, and took an oath of them, that they should do according to this promise. **Heb. 6:16** For men verily swear by the greater: and an oath for confirmation is to them an end of all strife. **17** Wherein God, willing more abundantly to shew unto the heirs of promise the immutability of his counsel, confirmed it by an oath.

39. Of Personal Propriety

WE DO BELIEVE that every man hath a just and peculiar right and propriety in his own goods, and that they are not common to others; yet we believe that every man is obliged to administer to the poor saints, and to the public interest of God, according to his ability, or as God hath blessed him.

> **Exod. 20:17** Thou shalt not covet thy neighbour's house, thou shalt not covet thy neighbour's wife, nor his manservant, nor his maidservant, nor his ox, nor his ass, nor any thing that is thy neighbour's. **Acts 5:4** Whiles it remained, was it not thine own? and after it was sold, was it not in thine own power? why hast thou conceived this thing in thine heart? thou hast not lied unto men, but unto God. **Acts 20:33** I have coveted no man's silver, or gold, or apparel.

POSTSCRIPT

THERE IS SOMETHING contained in the 13th article that may seem to want some explication, in these words (speaking of a man actually and personally justified) that his sins 'past, present, and to come' are all forgiven: We believing that if any sins of a justified person were afterwards charged upon him, it must of necessity make a breach in his unalterable and everlasting justification, which is but one act in God; hence 'There is … no condemnation to them which are in Christ Jesus' (Rom. 8:1): yet I find an able and worthy writer (Mr Thomas Gilbert) distinguisheth pardon of sin thus, viz.:

1. Fundamentally in Christ, as a common pardon of all the elect before faith, which lieth in Christ making full satisfaction for all their sins, meriting faith for them, etc.

2. Actual, of all the elect in Christ on believing; this actual pardon being nothing else but the actual possession in their own persons of their fundamental pardon in the person of Christ: And Dr Thomas Goodwin speaks to the same purpose, to which I agree. And that this actual pardon of the legal guilt is twofold.

1. Formal, of all their sins past, removing their legal guilt.

2. Virtual, of all their sins to come, preventing their legal guilt. Dr Ames speaks to the same purpose,[1] and many others. I cannot see

---

[1] Dr Ames saith, that not only the sins of a justified person that are past are remitted, but also in some sort those to come (Num. 23:25; John 5:24), yet he distinguishes between a formal

how a believer should be for ever formally justified from all sins past, present, and to come, and yet not formally pardoned.

This author which I have lately met with, distinguisheth well between legal guilt and gospel guilt; the first obliging to divine wrath, or eternal punishment; the latter, i.e. gospel guilt, obliging to gospel, or fatherly, chastisement for gospel sins. Now I see not but that as soon as a believer is personally justified, all his sins, though not yet committed, as to legal guilt, or vindictive wrath, i.e. that guilt that obliges to eternal condemnation, are pardoned, for the reason before.

Saith he, 'Virtual Pardon keeps off Legal Guilt where it would be.' To which I reply, if it be kept off, so that it never comes upon believers, then it follows they were actually pardoned before in that respect: yet he says, Sins cannot be said to be formally pardoned before formally committed; but says, 'no guilt can come upon them to condemnation, though new guilt'; yet no new legal guilt, because always justified. We see no hurt if his terms be admitted.

Objection. *What do believers then pray for, when they pray for the pardon of sin?*

Answer 1. That God would not chastise them sorely, or afflict them as a Father, according to the greatness of their offences.

2. That if his chastening hand is upon us, he would be pleased graciously to remove it.

3. That he would be pleased to clear up to our consciences, or give us the evidence of our pardon through Christ's merits, and that we may know we are complete in Christ, or without spot before the throne in our free justification.

4. Nay, believers are to pray to God to remove that Sin from them (saith this worthy author) whose desert of punishment cannot

---

and virtual pardon: Sins past, says he, are remitted in themselves; sins to come, in the subject or person sinning.

be removed from it; and to spread their sins before the Lord in the highest sense of the deepest demerit of all legal punishment, so that they may put the higher accent upon the free grace of God, and estimate upon the full satisfaction of Christ, whereby their persons are so fully freed from all actual obligation to any legal punishment, the whole and utmost whereof their sins deserve.

5. Moreover, that God would continue, and never revoke his most gracious pardon, till he pronounceth the final sentence of it at the day of judgment (as well this author notes), for a renewed sense and assurance of its grant and continuance: and thus to pray, saith he, there are both precepts and promises.